TO

_____

ON

_____

FROM

_____

EASTER TREASURY OF ILLUSTRATED BIBLE STORIES

MATT LOCKHART

General Editor

Kregel's Easter Treasury of Illustrated Bible Stories
© 2025 by Classic Bible Art, LLC

Published by Kregel Publications, a division of Kregel Inc., 2450 Oak Industrial Dr. NE, Grand Rapids, MI 49505. www.kregel.com.

All rights reserved. No part of this book may be reproduced; stored in a retrieval system, including but not limited to generative AI training systems; or transmitted in any form or by any means—for example, electronic, mechanical, photocopy, recording, or otherwise—without the publisher's prior written permission or by license agreement. The only exception is brief quotations in printed reviews.

Scripture quotations marked GNT are from the Good News Translation in Today's English Version—Second Edition Copyright © 1992 by American Bible Society. Used by Permission.

All Scripture marked with the designation GW is taken from GOD'S WORD®. © 1995, 2003, 2013, 2014, 2019, 2020 by God's Word to the Nations Mission Society. Used by permission.

Scripture marked ICB taken from the Holy Bible, International Children's Bible® Copyright © 1986, 1988, 1999, 2015 by Thomas Nelson. Used by permission. All rights reserved.

Scripture quotations marked NCV are from the New Century Version®. Copyright © 2005 by Thomas Nelson. Used by permission. All rights reserved.

Scripture quotations marked NIrV are taken from the Holy Bible, New International Reader's Version®, NIrV® Copyright © 1995, 1996, 1998, 2014 by Biblica, Inc.® Used by permission of Zondervan. All rights reserved worldwide. www.zondervan.com The "NIrV" and "New International Reader's Version" are trademarks registered in the United States Patent and Trademark Office by Biblica, Inc.®

Scripture quotations marked NLT are taken from the *Holy Bible*, New Living Translation, copyright ©1996, 2004, 2015 by Tyndale House Foundation. Used by permission of Tyndale House Publishers, Carol Stream, Illinois 60188. All rights reserved.

Library of Congress Cataloging-in-Publication Data
Names: Lockhart, Matthew, editor.
Title: Kregel's Easter treasury of illustrated bible stories / Matt Lockhart, general editor.
Other titles: Easter treasury of illustrated bible stories
Description: First edition. | Grand Rapids, MI : Kregel Publications, a division of Kregel Inc., [2025] | The wonderful illustrations featured throughout this volume come from one of the largest privately held collections of vintage Bible art.
Identifiers: LCCN 2024031649
Subjects: LCSH: Jesus Christ—Passion. | Easter. | Bible—Illustrations. | Bible stories.
Classification: LCC BT431.3 .K74 2025 | DDC 232.96—dc23/eng/20240801
LC record available at https://lccn.loc.gov/2024031649

ISBN 978-0-8254-4899-7

Printed in China

25 26 27 28 29 / 5 4 3 2 1

Contents

A Note to Parents	6
About the Artwork	7
Jesus Anointed	8
The Triumphal Entry	10
Jesus Washes the Disciples' Feet	12
The Last Supper	14
In the Garden of Gethsemane	16
Jesus Betrayed and Arrested	18
Jesus Before the High Priest	20
Peter Denies Jesus	22
Jesus Before Pilate	24
The Soldiers Beat and Mock Jesus	26
Jesus Rejected and Condemned	28
Jesus Bears the Cross	30
The Crucifixion	32
Jesus Laid to Rest	34
Jesus Rises to Life Again!	36
Peter and John Race to the Tomb	38
Jesus Appears to Mary Magdalene	40
The Ascension	42
Lenten Bible Reading Plan	45

A Note to Parents

Welcome to *Kregel's Easter Treasury of Illustrated Bible Stories*! I'm excited to share these wonderful stories and illustrations with you.

Inside these pages you will find eighteen episodes that encompass the key events surrounding the death and resurrection of Jesus. Each story in this family keepsake is attractively laid out and beautifully adorned with classic fine art. Additionally, there are "Easter Extras" included with each passage to help your family engage with the resurrection story in a deeper way. As a bonus, a Lenten Bible Reading Plan that you can follow leading up to Easter is available in the back of this book.

While many Bible storybooks retell stories, I have compiled text from actual Scripture! I have used a variety of respected modern translations to render each episode in a way that is easy to read and understand. The verses printed in this book are referenced at the end of each Scripture passage, along with the designated translation abbreviation as noted on the copyright page.

Since nothing can replace the value of reading from your own Bible, I encourage you to explore these stories further in the Word and in full context by reading for yourself the chapters from which the episodes are taken. Encourage your children or grandchildren to read the Bible independently as well. Starting this practice at a young age helps kids know God and establish the important habit of regular Bible reading.

Matt

About the Artwork

The wonderful illustrations featured throughout this volume come from one of the largest privately held collections of vintage Bible art. The art was originally commissioned by Standard Publishing, in pursuit of providing high-quality illustrations to complement their Sunday school materials. Some of the works featured in this book date back to more than one hundred years ago, as the collection came together over a period of about fifty years, with the latest pieces dating to the late 1950s.

Within the overall collection, there is artwork attributed to more than fifty different artists. Of the illustrations featured in this book, several were done by two American artists, Cleveland Woodward and Otto Stemler.

Cleveland Woodward (1900–1985): Born in Glendale, Ohio, and a graduate of the Art Academy of Cincinnati, Cleveland continued his training in Europe, studying at the British Academy of Arts in Rome. He also spent time in the Holy Land and was known for his Bible illustrations.

Otto Stemler (1872–1953): Born in Cincinnati, Ohio, Otto studied at the Art Academy of Cincinnati and was Standard's primary in-house artist. He made artistic contributions to the collection over the span of a forty-year career. His works often feature bold colors.

Matt Lockhart has spent over three decades in ministry and Christian publishing and enjoys creating books that help children and adults get into the Bible.

Jesus Anointed

Six days before the Passover Feast, Jesus went to Bethany, where Lazarus lived. (Lazarus is the man Jesus raised from death.) There they had a dinner for Jesus. Martha served the food. Lazarus was one of the people eating with Jesus. Mary brought in a pint of very expensive perfume made from pure nard. She poured the perfume on Jesus' feet, and then she wiped his feet with her hair. And the sweet smell from the perfume filled the whole house.

John 12:1–3 (ICB)

In the forty days leading up to Easter, consider using the Lenten Bible Reading Plan on page 45.

The Triumphal Entry

On the next day the large crowd that had come to the Passover festival heard that Jesus was coming to Jerusalem. So they took palm branches and went to meet him. They were shouting,

> "Hosanna!
> Blessed is the one who comes in the name of the Lord,
> the king of Israel!"

Jesus obtained a donkey and sat on it, as Scripture says:

> "Don't be afraid, people of Zion!
> Your king is coming.
> He is riding on a donkey's colt."

John 12:12–15 (GW)

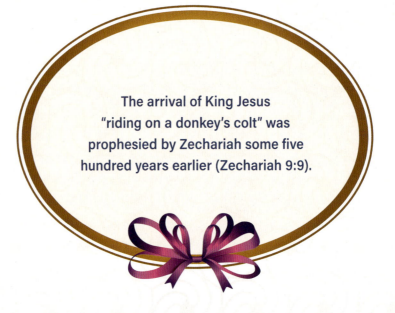

The arrival of King Jesus "riding on a donkey's colt" was prophesied by Zechariah some five hundred years earlier (Zechariah 9:9).

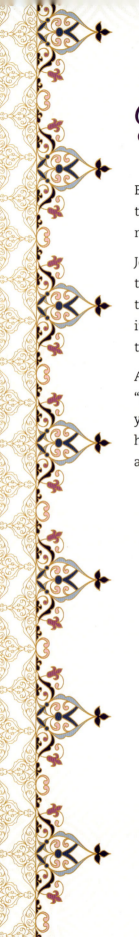

Jesus Washes the Disciples' Feet

Before the Passover celebration, Jesus knew that his hour had come to leave this world and return to his Father. He had loved his disciples during his ministry on earth, and now he loved them to the very end.

Jesus knew that the Father had given him authority over everything and that he had come from God and would return to God. So he got up from the table, took off his robe, wrapped a towel around his waist, and poured water into a basin. Then he began to wash the disciples' feet, drying them with the towel he had around him.

After washing their feet, he put on his robe again and sat down and asked, "Do you understand what I was doing? You call me 'Teacher' and 'Lord,' and you are right, because that's what I am. And since I, your Lord and Teacher, have washed your feet, you ought to wash each other's feet. I have given you an example to follow. Do as I have done to you."

John 13:1, 3–5, 12–15 (NLT)

> Passover is an annual celebration observed by Jewish people to remember when Israel was rescued from slavery in Egypt, as recorded in the book of Exodus.

The Last Supper

While they were eating, Jesus took bread. He gave thanks and broke it. He handed it to his disciples and said, "Take this and eat it. This is my body."

Then he took a cup. He gave thanks and handed it to them. He said, "All of you drink from it. This is my blood of the covenant. It is poured out to forgive the sins of many people."

Then they sang a hymn and went out to the Mount of Olives.

Matthew 26:26–28, 30 (NIrV)

According to Jewish tradition, the hymn sung by Jesus and the disciples was the Hallel, which includes Psalms 113-118. *Hallel* is a Hebrew word that means "praise."

In the Garden of Gethsemane

Then Jesus went with his followers to a place called Gethsemane. He said to them, "Sit here while I go over there and pray." He took Peter and the two sons of Zebedee with him, and he began to be very sad and troubled. He said to them, "My heart is full of sorrow, to the point of death. Stay here and watch with me."

After walking a little farther away from them, Jesus fell to the ground and prayed, "My Father, if it is possible, do not give me this cup of suffering. But do what you want, not what I want." Then Jesus went back to his followers and found them asleep. He said to Peter, "You men could not stay awake with me for one hour?"

Matthew 26:36–40 (NCV)

The "sons of Zebedee" were the disciples James and John, brothers who were nicknamed Sons of Thunder by Jesus (Mark 3:17).

Jesus Betrayed and Arrested

Judas, one of the twelve disciples, arrived with a crowd of men armed with swords and clubs. They had been sent by the leading priests and elders of the people. The traitor, Judas, had given them a prearranged signal: "You will know which one to arrest when I greet him with a kiss." So Judas came straight to Jesus. "Greetings, Rabbi!" he exclaimed and gave him the kiss.

Jesus said, "My friend, go ahead and do what you have come for."

Matthew 26:47–50 (NLT)

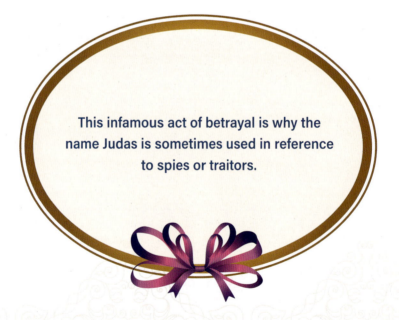

This infamous act of betrayal is why the name Judas is sometimes used in reference to spies or traitors.

Jesus Before the High Priest

Those men who arrested Jesus led him to the house of Caiaphas, the high priest. The teachers of the law and the Jewish elders were gathered there. Peter followed Jesus but did not go near him. He followed Jesus to the courtyard of the high priest's house. He sat down with the guards to see what would happen to Jesus.

The leading priests and the Jewish council tried to find something false against Jesus so that they could kill him.

Matthew 26:57–59 (ICB)

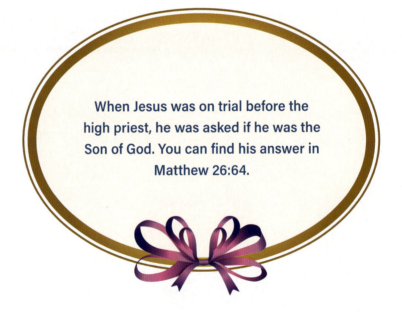

When Jesus was on trial before the high priest, he was asked if he was the Son of God. You can find his answer in Matthew 26:64.

Peter Denies Jesus

Peter was sitting out in the courtyard. A female servant came to him. "You also were with Jesus of Galilee," she said.

But in front of all of them, Peter said he was not. "I don't know what you're talking about," he said.

Then he went out to the gate leading into the courtyard. There another servant saw him. She said to the people, "This fellow was with Jesus of Nazareth."

Again he said he was not. With a curse he said, "I don't know the man!"

After a little while, those standing there went up to Peter. "You must be one of them," they said. "The way you talk gives you away."

Then Peter began to curse and said to them, "I don't know the man!"

Right away a rooster crowed. Then Peter remembered what Jesus had said. "The rooster will crow," Jesus had told him. "Before it does, you will say three times that you don't know me." Peter went outside. He broke down and cried.

Matthew 26:69–75 (NIrV)

Find the rooster in the painting. God used this common bird to remind Peter of what Jesus had told him in the upper room (Mark 14:27-31).

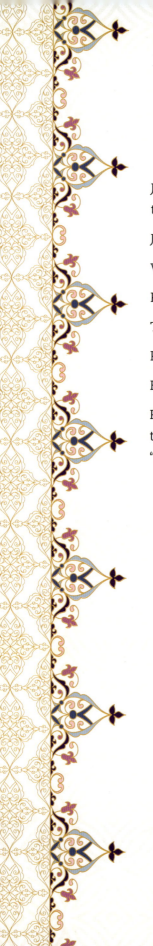

Jesus Before Pilate

Jesus stood before Pilate the governor. Pilate asked him, "Are you the King of the Jews?"

Jesus answered, "Yes, I am."

When the leading priests and the elders accused Jesus, he said nothing.

Pilate asked, "What should I do with Jesus, the one called the Christ?"

They all answered, "Kill him on a cross!"

Pilate asked, "Why do you want me to kill him? What wrong has he done?"

But they shouted louder, "Kill him on a cross!"

Pilate saw that he could do nothing about this, and a riot was starting. So he took some water and washed his hands in front of the crowd. Then he said, "I am not guilty of this man's death. You are the ones who are causing it!"

Matthew 27:11–12, 22–24 (ICB)

Pilate was a Roman government official. He oversaw the province of Judea and was its governor.

The Soldiers Beat and Mock Jesus

Then Pilate ordered that Jesus be taken away and whipped. The soldiers made a crown from some thorny branches and put it on Jesus' head and put a purple robe around him. Then they came to him many times and said, "Hail, King of the Jews!" and hit him in the face.

John 19:1–3 (NCV)

> The Roman practice of whipping was also called flogging or scourging. A soldier would use a short whip (called a *flagrum*) consisting of multiple leather strips.

Jesus Rejected and Condemned

Once more Pilate came out. He said to the Jews gathered there, "Look, I am bringing Jesus out to you. I want to let you know that I find no basis for a charge against him." Jesus came out wearing the crown of thorns and the purple robe. Then Pilate said to them, "Here is the man!"

As soon as the chief priests and their officials saw him, they shouted, "Crucify him! Crucify him!"

But Pilate answered, "You take him and crucify him. I myself find no basis for a charge against him."

But they shouted, "Take him away! Take him away! Crucify him!"

John 19:4–6, 15 (NIrV)

From the expressions on the faces of the people in the crowd, how do you think they were feeling? How does this story make you feel?

Jesus Bears the Cross

Finally, Pilate handed Jesus over to them to be nailed to a cross.

So the soldiers took charge of Jesus. He had to carry his own cross. He went out to a place called the Skull. In the Aramaic language it was called Golgotha.

John 19:16–17 (NIrV)

The gospels of Matthew, Mark, and Luke tell us that the soldiers forced a man named Simon (of Cyrene) to help Jesus carry the cross. Simon was the father of two boys—Alexander and Rufus (Mark 15:21).

The Crucifixion

When they had nailed him to the cross, they divided up his clothes by casting lots. They sat down and kept watch over him there. Above his head they placed the written charge against him. It read,

This is Jesus, the King of the Jews.

From noon until three o'clock, the whole land was covered with darkness. About three o'clock, Jesus cried out in a loud voice. He said, "*Eli, Eli, lema sabachthani?*" This means "My God, my God, why have you deserted me?"

After Jesus cried out again in a loud voice, he died.

Matthew 27:35–37, 45–46, 50 (NIrV)

The sign that Pilate posted on the cross was written in three different languages: Aramaic, Latin, and Greek.

Jesus Laid to Rest

In the evening a rich man named Joseph arrived. He was from the city of Arimathea and had become a disciple of Jesus. He went to Pilate and asked for the body of Jesus. Pilate ordered that it be given to him.

Joseph took the body and wrapped it in a clean linen cloth. Then he laid it in his own new tomb, which had been cut in a rock. After rolling a large stone against the door of the tomb, he went away.

Matthew 27:57–60 (GW)

> Joseph of Arimathea was a member of the council (the Sanhedrin), but he did not consent to the action the council took against Jesus (Mark 15:43; Luke 23:50-51).

Jesus Rises to Life Again!

After the Sabbath was over, Mary Magdalene, Mary the mother of James, and Salome bought spices to go and anoint the body of Jesus. Very early on Sunday morning, at sunrise, they went to the tomb. On the way they said to one another, "Who will roll away the stone for us from the entrance to the tomb?" (It was a very large stone.) Then they looked up and saw that the stone had already been rolled back. So they entered the tomb, where they saw a young man sitting at the right, wearing a white robe—and they were alarmed.

"Don't be alarmed," he said. "I know you are looking for Jesus of Nazareth, who was crucified. He is not here—he has been raised! Look, here is the place where he was placed."

Mark 16:1–6 (GNT)

Eggs have been used as an Easter symbol by Christians for centuries. They represent new life (the hatching and emergence of a chick), and the hollow shell reminds us of the empty tomb.

Peter and John Race to the Tomb

Early on Sunday morning, while it was still dark, Mary Magdalene went to the tomb and saw that the stone had been taken away from the entrance. She went running to Simon Peter and the other disciple, whom Jesus loved, and told them, "They have taken the Lord from the tomb, and we don't know where they have put him!"

Then Peter and the other disciple went to the tomb. The two of them were running, but the other disciple ran faster than Peter and reached the tomb first. He bent over and saw the linen cloths, but he did not go in. Behind him came Simon Peter, and he went straight into the tomb. He saw the linen cloths lying there and the cloth which had been around Jesus' head. It was not lying with the linen cloths but was rolled up by itself. Then the other disciple, who had reached the tomb first, also went in; he saw and believed.

John 20:1–8 (GNT)

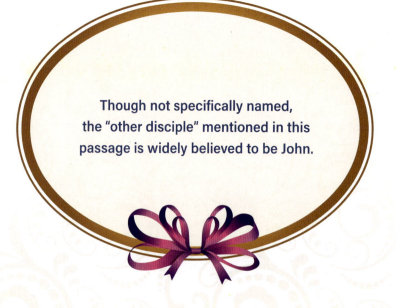

Though not specifically named, the "other disciple" mentioned in this passage is widely believed to be John.

Jesus Appears to Mary Magdalene

Mary was standing outside the tomb crying, and as she wept, she stooped and looked in. She saw two white-robed angels, one sitting at the head and the other at the foot of the place where the body of Jesus had been lying. "Dear woman, why are you crying?" the angels asked her.

"Because they have taken away my Lord," she replied, "and I don't know where they have put him."

She turned to leave and saw someone standing there. It was Jesus, but she didn't recognize him. "Dear woman, why are you crying?" Jesus asked her. "Who are you looking for?"

She thought he was the gardener. "Sir," she said, "if you have taken him away, tell me where you have put him, and I will go and get him."

"Mary!" Jesus said.

She turned to him and cried out, "Rabboni!" (which is Hebrew for "Teacher").

Mary Magdalene found the disciples and told them, "I have seen the Lord!"

John 20:11–16, 18 (NLT)

A traditional Easter greeting among Christians is "He is risen!" with the response of either "He is risen indeed!" or "Indeed He is risen!"

The Ascension

Jesus led his followers out of Jerusalem almost to Bethany. He raised his hands and blessed them. While he was blessing them, he was separated from them and carried into heaven.

Luke 24:50–51 (ICB)

The gospel of Mark tells us that before returning to the Father in heaven, Jesus told his disciples, "Go everywhere in the world, and tell the Good News to everyone" (Mark 16:15 NCV).

Easter shows us how much God loves us, and it is a celebration of Jesus's victory over sin and death. God wants you to know the good news—that he sent Jesus for you! Jesus loves you and wants you to believe and follow him. Romans 10:9 says, "If you confess that Jesus is Lord and believe that God raised him from death, you will be saved" (GNT). If you're not sure what this means, talk about it with your mom or dad or someone you know who loves Jesus.

Together you can pray something like this:
Dear God, thank you for sending Jesus to earth to die on the cross, take away our sins, and rise to life again, all so we can have life forever in heaven someday. Jesus, I'm sorry for my sins. I want to live my life following you. Please come into my heart as my Savior. Amen.

Lenten Bible Reading Plan

Read the forty short Bible passages below between Ash Wednesday and Easter Sunday. Reading these verses together as a family will help prepare your hearts for Resurrection Sunday!

Day 1: Joel 2:12–17
Day 2: Isaiah 58:1–10
Day 3: Matthew 6:1–4, 16–18
Day 4: Psalm 103:1–6
Day 5: Psalm 103:8–18
Day 6: Acts 2:22–24
Day 7: Psalm 16:7–11
Day 8: Acts 2:29–36
Day 9: Acts 13:26–33
Day 10: Acts 13:36–39
Day 11: Genesis 22:1–8
Day 12: Genesis 22:9–14
Day 13: Romans 8:28–39
Day 14: Mark 1:9–15
Day 15: Luke 4:14–21
Day 16: Romans 5:12–19
Day 17: Romans 4:13–25
Day 18: Romans 5:1–11
Day 19: Mark 8:27–31
Day 20: Mark 8:34–38
Day 21: Mark 9:2–10
Day 22: Philippians 3:1–11
Day 23: Philippians 3:12–21
Day 24: Luke 13:31–33
Day 25: 2 Timothy 2:1–10
Day 26: 1 Corinthians 1:18–25
Day 27: John 3:1–13
Day 28: John 3:14–21
Day 29: 2 Corinthians 5:11–21
Day 30: Ephesians 2:1–10
Day 31: John 12:1–8
Day 32: John 12:12–16
Day 33: Matthew 26:17–29
Day 34: Matthew 26:36–46
Day 35: John 19:17–22
Day 36: John 19:23–30
Day 37: Mark 16:1–7
Day 38: Matthew 28:16–20
Day 39: 2 Corinthians 5:14–21
Day 40: Psalm 118:14–24

Continue the Tradition

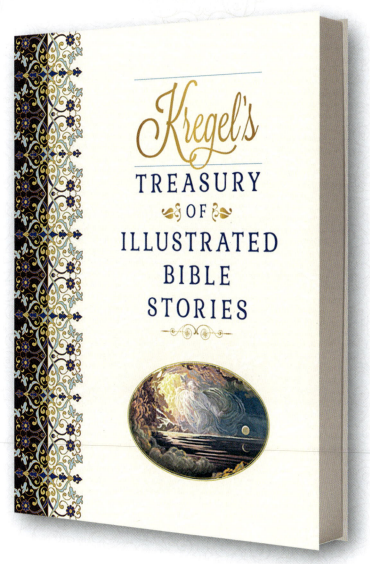

This richly designed, high-quality hardcover is ideal for Easter, kindergarten graduations, baptisms, and other gift-giving occasions. With 250 stories pulled straight from the text of Scripture, *Kregel's Treasury of Illustrated Bible Stories* is destined to become a cherished family classic.

A Treasury for Christmas!

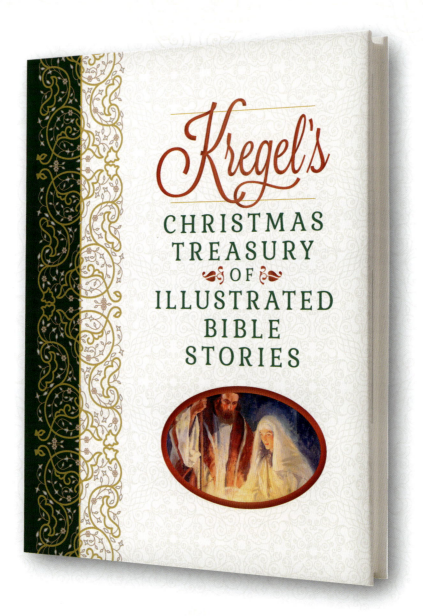

Experience God's greatest gift through the Christmas story in Scripture and beloved classic art—a perfect family tradition.